The Book Of Hermes Or Thoth

Arthur Edward Waite

Kessinger Publishing's Rare Reprints

Thousands of Scarce and Hard-to-Find Books on These and other Subjects!

- Americana
- Ancient Mysteries
- Animals
- Anthropology
- Architecture
- Arts
- Astrology
- Bibliographies
- Biographies & Memoirs
- Body, Mind & Spirit
- Business & Investing
- Children & Young Adult
- Collectibles
- Comparative Religions
- Crafts & Hobbies
- Earth Sciences
- Education
- Ephemera
- Fiction
- Folklore
- Geography
- Health & Diet
- History
- Hobbies & Leisure
- Humor
- Illustrated Books
- Language & Culture
- Law
- Life Sciences
- Literature
- Medicine & Pharmacy
- Metaphysical
- Music
- Mystery & Crime
- Mythology
- Natural History
- Outdoor & Nature
- Philosophy
- Poetry
- Political Science
- Science
- Psychiatry & Psychology
- Reference
- Religion & Spiritualism
- Rhetoric
- Sacred Books
- Science Fiction
- Science & Technology
- Self-Help
- Social Sciences
- Symbolism
- Theatre & Drama
- Theology
- Travel & Explorations
- War & Military
- Women
- Yoga
- *Plus Much More!*

**We kindly invite you to view our catalog list at:
http://www.kessinger.net**

THIS ARTICLE WAS EXTRACTED FROM THE BOOK:

Mysteries of Magic: A Digest of the Writings of Eliphas Levi

BY THIS AUTHOR:

Arthur Edward Waite

ISBN 1564593746

READ MORE ABOUT THE BOOK AT OUR WEB SITE:

http://www.kessinger.net

OR ORDER THE COMPLETE
BOOK FROM YOUR FAVORITE STORE

ISBN 1564593746

Because this article has been extracted from a parent book, it may have non-pertinent text at the beginning or end of it.

Any blank pages following the article are necessary for our book production requirements. The article herein is complete.

Kabbalistical and astrological calculations, puerile, possibly, and completely arbitrary, if made without inspiration, by cold curiosity, and without a powerful will.

III.—The Book of Hermes or of Thoth.

Among the sacred books of the Christians are two works which the infallible Church never ventures to explain, and does not pretend to understand—the prophecy of Ezekiel, and the Apocalypse—two Kabbalistic claviculæ, doubtless reserved by heaven for the commentaries of magian kings, books which for faithful believers are sealed with seven seals, yet are perfectly clear to the infidel who is an initiate of the occult sciences.

There exists also another book, but this, though in a certain sense it is popular and found everywhere, is of all the most hidden and unknown, because it is the key of all the rest; it is in circulation without being known by the public, where it is, no one expects to discover it, and should anyone divine its existence, he would a thousand times over vainly waste his time if he sought it under any but one form. This book, more ancient perhaps than that of Enoch, has never been translated, and it exists only in primitive characters, on single leaves, like the tablets of antiquity. A distinguished scholar has revealed, though no one appears to have noticed it, not exactly its secret but its antiquity and extraordinary preservation: another scholar, though of a genius more fantastic than judicious, passed thirty years in the study of this book, and has barely divined its importance. It is, in truth, a monumental and phenomenal work, strong and simple as the architecture of the Pyramids, and durable, therefore, as are those; a book which epitomizes all sciences while its infinite combinations can solve all problems; a book which speaks by evoking thought, the inspirer and controller of all possible conceptions, the masterpiece perhaps of the human mind, and undoubtedly one of the finest things which antiquity has bequeathed to us, a universal *clavicula*, the name of which was understood and explained by the learned *illuminé*, William Postel; a unique text, of which the first characters alone ravished into ecstasy the devotional spirit of

Saint Martin, and might have restored reason to the sublime and unfortunate Swedenborg.

The universal key of magical arts is the key of all ancient religious dogmas, the key of the Kabbalah and the Bible, the primitive source of divine and human tradition, the clavicula of Solomon. Now, this clavicula or little key, looked on as lost for centuries, has been recovered by us, and we have been enabled to open the sepulchres of the elder world, to make the dead speak, to behold the monuments of the past in all their splendour, to understand all the enigmas of the past, and penetrate into every sanctuary. The use of this key was, among the ancients, permitted only to the high priests, and its secret was confided to the flower of the initiates alone. This key consisted of a hieroglyphical and numeral alphabet, giving expression to a series of universal and absolute ideas by means of characters and numbers; then came a scale of ten numbers multiplied by four symbols and bound together by twelve figures, representing the twelve signs of the zodiac, plus four genii, those of the four cardinal points.

The symbolic tetrad, represented in the mysteries of Memphis and Thebes by the four forms of the sphinx, the man, the eagle, the bull, and the lion, corresponded with the four elements of the old world—water being signified by the chalice which the man or aquarius holds; air by the circle or nimbus which surrounds the head of the celestial eagle; fire by the wood which feeds it, by the tree which the heat of the sun and earth fructifies, and lastly by the sceptre of royalty, of which the lion is the emblem; earth by the sword of Mithra, who annually immolates the sacred bull and pours out with its blood the sap which swells in all the fruits of the earth.

Now, these four signs, with their analogies, are the explanation of the one word hidden in every sanctuary, of that word which the bacchantes seemed to divine, when, during the celebration of the feasts of Iacchos, they were exalted into delirium for the glory of Io EVOHE! What then was meant by this mysterious word? It was the name of the four primitive letters of the mother tongue: the JOD, symbol of the vine-stock or paternal sceptre of Noah; the HE, symbol of the chalice of libations; the VAU, which joins the preceding signs, and was represented in India by the great and mysterious lingam. Such, in the divine word, was the three-fold sign of the triad; then the maternal letter appeared a second time to express the fecundity of nature and woman, to formulate also the dogma of universal and progressive analogies, descending from causes to effects and remounting from effects to causes. The sacred word, moreover, was not pronounced; it was spelt and read off in four words, which are the four sacred words: JOD HE VAU HE.

In the sixteenth century, a man of exalted faith and wide erudition had discovered the key of all religious mysteries and published a small work: *Clavis Absconditorum à Constitutione Mundi*, "The Key of Things kept Secret from the Foundation of the World." This man was an illuminate Hebraist and Kabbalist, named William Postel.[1] He believed that he had found the true signification of the Tetragram in a hieroglyphic book anterior to the Bible, and termed by him the Genesis of Enoch, doubtless to conceal its real name from the uninitiated; for on the ring of his symbolic key, the representation of which he gives as an occult explanation of his singular work, he thus traces his mysterious tetrad:—

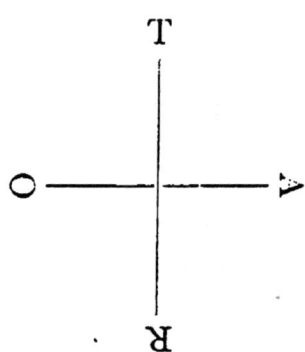

forming in this manner a word which, read from left to right beginning at the bottom, makes ROTA, by beginning at the top, makes TARO, and even TAROT, if the initial letter be repeated to mark the circle more distinctly, and read from

[1] He was born in the Diocese of Avranches and was so precocious that he was made *maître d'école* at the age of fourteen. He visited the far East, and died in 1581, being ninety-six years old. He was persuaded that the King of France was destined to universal monarchy as the lineal descendant of Noah's eldest son.

right to left, as Hebrew should be read, makes TORA, the sacramental name which the Jews give to their sacred book.

Let us compare with this enigma of Postel the erudite observations made by Court de Gebelin, in the sixth volume of his *Monde Primitif*, concerning a book of the ancient Egyptians, which has come down to our own times under the futile pretext of a game of cards: let us examine the mysterious figures of these cards, of which the first twenty-two are evidently a hieroglyphic alphabet, where symbols are explained by numbers, while the entire game is divided into four tens, each accompanied by four figures with four colours and four different symbols, and we shall have the right to ask if the Tarot of the Bohemians be not the Genesis of Enoch, the Taro, Rota, or Tora of William Postel, and his initiates the true Hebrew Kabbalists! If in this state of doubt we penetrate the learned obscurities of the Zohar, the great sacred book of the supreme Kabbalah, our conjectures will soon change into certitude when we learn that the Jod, the tenth and principal letter of the Hebrew alphabet, has been always regarded by initiated Kabbalists as the sign of the First Cause, represented by the Egyptian phallus and by the rod of Moses; that the He, the second letter of the name of יהוה and the fifth of the alphabet, signifies the passive and demonstrative form of the active principle, and corresponds to the cteïs of ancient sacred hieroglyphs; that the Vau, the third letter of the Tetragram, and the sixth of the alphabet, signifies crook, entanglement, attraction, and corresponds to the hieroglyphic signs of the cross, the sword, and the lingam, as we have before said; finally, that the He, repeated at the end of the Tetragram, possibly represented the circle which would result from the superposition of two cups, one upright, the other inverted. We have then the key of the denary symbols of the Tarot, the first of which represents a blossoming rod, the second a royal chalice, the third a sword piercing a crown, and the fourth a circle enclosing a lotos flower.

It remains for us, in order to be fully initiated into the mysteries of the Genesis of Postel, to thoroughly understand the series of absolute theological and philosophical ideas which the ancients attached to the ten first numbers. Here Pythagoras is in agreement with the depositaries of the secret of Moses, for they have all drawn from the same fountain; and we have seen that in the tetrad the secret signs of the supreme Kabbalah express precisely the same doctrine as the hieroglyphs of Egypt and the sacred symbols of India. The phallus, the cteïs, the lingam of life, the sceptre of Osiris, the cup or flower of Isis, the lingam of Horus and the cycle of Hermes, Aaron's blossoming rod, the patera which contains the manna, the sacrificial sword and the dish for offerings, the pontifical staff, the eucharistic chalice, the Cross and the Divine Host, all religious signs, correspond to the four hieroglyphic symbols of the Tarot, which are the hieratic explanation of the four letters of the great and Divine Tetragram.

What most attracted the attention of Court de Gebelin when he discovered the Tarot, were the hieroglyphs of the twenty-first card, entitled the World. This card, which is no other than the identical key of William Postel, represents Truth naked and victorious in the centre of a crown which is divided into four parts by four lotus flowers. At the four corners of the card are seen the four emblematic animals which are the analysis of the sphinx, which St John borrowed from the prophet Ezekiel, as Ezekiel himself had borrowed them from the bucephalous or other sphinxes of Egypt and Assyria. These four figures, which a tradition, incomprehensible to the Church herself, still gives as the attributes of our four evangelists, represent the four elementary forms of the Kabbalah, the four seasons, the four metals, and lastly the four mysterious letters of the Jewish TORA, of Ezekiel's wheel, ROTA, and of the TAROT which, according to Postel, is the key of things hidden from the beginning of the world. It must be also remarked that the word Tarot is composed of the sacred letters of the monogram of Constantine—a Greek P crossed by a T between the Alpha and the Omega, which signify the beginning and the end. Disposed in this manner, it is a word analogous to the INRI of the Freemasons, wherein the two I's express equally the beginning and the end, since in the Kabbalah the Iod and all its derivations are symbolic of the phallus and of creation; the beginning and the end, expressed thus by the same letter, give the notion of the eternal evolution of the divine cycle, and therein the INRI is more profound, and belongs to a higher grade of initiation than the Tarot.

If we compare the hieroglyphic form of the Cross in the primitive Church with these discoveries, we shall be struck by many additional analogies. The first Christians usually composed the Cross from the four segments of the circle. I have seen one with ten branches issuing from one another, and four rivers at its root; a copy may be found in the Latin work of Bosius on the triumph of the Cross. The first crosses were without Christ, and sometimes bore a dove with the inscription, INRI, to suggest that there is a concealed sense in this inscription, and that it is the province of the Holy Spirit to make us understand it. The four Kabbalistic animals are also frequently found at the four arms of the Cross, which thus becomes a philosophical emblem of the tetrad.

Those who doubt what we advance here may consult the Gnostic yet orthodox writings attributed to St Dionysius the Areopagite, and those of St Irenæus, Synesius, and Clement of Alexandria. But without leaving the canon of the New Testament, they will find in the Apocalypse an ample magical and kabbalistical clavicula, which appears to have been devised according to the numbers, symbols, and hieroglyphic figures of the Tarot. There, in fact, we find the sceptres, chalices, swords, and crowns, disposed by determined numbers and corresponding to each other by means of the denary and sacred septenary; there we find the four kings of the four quarters of the world, and the four horsemen which figure in our ordinary cards; we find the winged woman, and the Logos in kingly garments, afterwards in pontifical costume with several diadems on His tiara. Finally, the Apocalyptic key, which is the vision of Heaven, is identical with the number twenty-one of the Tarot, and reveals to us a throne surrounded by a double rainbow, and at the four corners of this crown the four sacramental animals of the Kabbalah. These coincidences are, at least, very curious, and afford much food for thought.

Enraptured by his discovery, Postel naïvely imagined that he possessed the bond of universal religious concord, and the future tranquillity of the world. It was at this period that he wrote his *Traité de la Concord Universelle*, his book on the *Raisons d'être du Saint Esprit*, and that he dedicated to the fathers of the Council of Trent, then assembled, the *Clavi absconditorum à constitutione Mundi*. The epistle he addresse them is curious :—he poses frankly as a prophet, and declares to the bishops and doctors that their anathemas are unseasonable since all men must ultimately be saved, this being the consequence he draws from the unity and perpetuity of analogica and rational revelation in the world.

The fathers of the council did not even do him the honou of chastising him. His book and letter were looked on as the productions of a madman and remained unanswered; bu a little later on, having advanced some propositions on the redemption of the human race which appeared to be heterodox he was shut up in a monastery, wherein he died in the convic tion that he should rise again to explain to men his grea discovery of the keys of the occult world and the mysteries o the Tetragram; for it seemed to him impossible that such revelation could be wholly lost to posterity.

The erudite Gaffarel had no doubt that the Theraphim c the Hebrews, by means of which they consulted the Urim an Thummim, were the figures of the four Kabbalistic animal: the symbols of which were summarized, as we shall presentl show, by the sphinxes or cherubim of the Ark. But he cite in connection with the usurped Theraphim of Michas, a curiou passage of Philo, which is an entire revelation on the ancier and sacerdotal origin of our Tarots. Gaffarel expresses hin self as follows: "He (Philo the Jew) says, speaking of th history concealed in the before-mentioned chapter of Judge: that Michas made of fine gold and silver three figures of youn boys and three young calves, in addition to a lion, an eagle, dragon, and a dove, in such a manner that if any one sougl him to learn a secret concerning his wife, he interrogated b the dove; if touching his children, by the young boy; if fc wealth, by the eagle; if for power or authority, by the lion; for fecundity, by the cherub or calf; if for length of days, b the dragon." This revelation of Philo, though treated lightl by Gaffarel, is of palmary importance to us. Here, in fact, w have the key of the tetrad, the figures of the four symboli animals in the twenty-first key of the Tarot, or the third septenary, thus repeating and epitomizing all the symbolism expressed by the three superposed septenaries; next the antagonism of colours signified by the dove and the dragon; then the circle or ROTA, formed by the dragon or serpent to express longevity; finally, the Kabbalistic divination of the complete Tarot, as it was afterwards practised by the Egyptian Bohemians, whose secrets were imperfectly divined and recovered by Etteilla.

We find in the Bible that the high priests consulted the Lord on the golden table of the holy Ark, between the cherubim, or bull-head and eagle-winged sphinxes, and that they consulted by means of the Theraphim, by the Urim, the Thummim, and the Ephod. The Ephod, as we know, was a magic square of twelve numbers and twelve words graven on precious stones. The word *Theraphim* in Hebrew means hieroglyphs or symbolical signs; the Urim and Thummim were the above and below, the east and west, the yea and nay, and these signs corresponded to the two columns of the Temple, Jakin and Bohas. When, therefore, the high priest wished to elicit an oracle, he drew by lot the Theraphim, or golden plates which bore the images of the four sacred words, and placed them in threes round the breastplate or Ephod, between the Urim and Thummim, that is, between the two onyxes which served as the clasps to the chains of the Ephod. The right onyx signified Gedulah, or mercy and magnificence, the left corresponded to Geburah, and signified justice and wrath; and if, for example, the sign of the lion was found near the stone where the name of the tribe of Judah was engraved, on the left side, the high priest would interpret the oracle thus: "The rod of the Lord is provoked against Judah." If the Theraphim represented the man, or the chalice, and were also found on the left, near the stone of Benjamin, the high priest would read: "The mercy of the Lord is wearied by the offences of Benjamin, which outrage Him in His love. For this reason will He pour forth on him the chalice of His indignation, &c." When the sovereign priesthood ceased in Israel; when all the oracles of the world were silenced in the presence of the Word made flesh and speaking by the mouth of the most popular and the mildest of sages; when the ark was lost, the sanctuary profaned, and the Temple destroyed, the mysteries of the Ephod and the Theraphim, no longer traced on gold and precious stones, were written, or rather drawn by some erudite Kabbalists on ivory, on parchment, or silvered or gilt copper, then, lastly, on simple cards, which were always suspected by the official Church as containing a dangerous key to her mysteries. Thence have come those Tarots the antiquity of which, revealed to the learned Court de Gebelin by the science of numbers and hieroglyphics itself, so much exercised at a later period the questionable perspicacity but persevering investigation of Etteilla.

Etteilla or Alliette, an *illuminé* hair-dresser, exclusively engrossed by his divinatory system, and the emolument he could derive from it, neither proficient in his own language nor even in orthography, pretended to reform, and thus attribute to himself, the Book of Thoth. On the Tarot which he published, which has become very scarce, we find the following naïve advertisement: "Etteilla, professor of Algebra, reformer of Cartomancy, and correctors (*sic*) of the modern *inaccuracies* of the ancient Book of Thoth, lives in the Rue de l'Oseille, No. 48 à Paris." Etteilla would have certainly done wisely not to have corrected the *inaccuracies* of which he speaks; his works have caused the ancient book discovered by Court de Gebelin to descend into the region of common magic and fortune-telling. He proves nothing who tries to prove too much, says an axiom of logic; of this Etteilla is another example, but his efforts, nevertheless, led him to a certain acquaintance with the Kabbalah, as may be seen in some rare passages of his unreadable works.

The true initiates, contemporaries of Etteilla, the Rosicrucians, for example, and the Martinists, who were in possession of the real Tarot, as is proved by a book of St Martin, where the divisions are those of the Tarot, and the following passage written by an enemy of the Rosicrucians: "They claim to possess a volume wherein they can learn all that is to be found in other books which now are or indeed can ever come into existence. This volume is their own reason, in which they find the prototype of all that subsists by their facility in analyzing, summarizing, and creating a kind of intellectual world and of all possible beings. See the philosophical, theosophical, and microcosmic cards "—(" Conspiracy against the Catholic Religion and against Crowned Heads," by the author of "The Veil raised for the Curious." Paris, Crapard, 1792)—the true initiates, we repeat, who included the secret of the Tarot among their greatest mysteries, were far from protesting against the errors of Etteilla, and left him to re-veil, not reveal, the arcanum of the veritable claviculæ of Solomon. So is it not without profound astonishment that we have recovered intact and unknown this key of all the doctrines and all the philosophies of the elder world. I speak of it as a key, and such it truly is, having the circle of four decades for its ring, and for its trunk or body the scale of twenty-two characters, then the three degrees of the triad for its wards, as Postel understood and represented it in his "Key of Things kept Secret from the Foundation of the World."

Without the Tarot, the magic of the ancients is to us a sealed book, and it is impossible to penetrate any of the great mysteries of the Kabbalah. It is, in fact, the hieroglyphic book of the thirty-two Kabbalistic paths, and its summary explanation is found in the Sepher Jetzirah, a work attributed to the patriarch Abraham. It only provides the interpretation of the magic squares of Agrippa and Paracelsus, as we may prove by forming these same squares with the keys of the Tarot, and by reading the hieroglyphs which will thus be found collected.

The seven magical squares of the planetary genii are, according to Paracelsus, as follows :—

Saturn.

2	9	4
7	5	3
6	1	8

Jupiter.

6	12	12	10
5	10	11	11
9	6	7	12
14	6	4	1

Mars.

14	10	22	22	18
20	12	7	20	2
8	17	9	9	8
12	3	9	5	26
11	23	8	6	11

The Sun.

9	22	1	32	25	19
7	11	27	18	8	3
19	14	16	15	23	24
18	20	22	21	17	13
22	29	10	19	26	12
36	5	35	6	12	13

THE SCIENCE OF THE PROPHETS

Venus.

22	47	18	41	0	35	8
25	23	47	17	42	11	29
10	6	14	9	18	36	12
3	31	16	25	43	19	37
38	14	32	31	26	44	20
21	39	8	33	22	27	45
46	15	40	19	24	03	27

Mercury.

8	52	39	5	24	61	66	11
49	15	14	52	52	12	10	56
41	43	22	14	45	19	18	48
33	34	35	29	20	38	39	25
40	6	27	59	31	30	31	33
17	47	55	28	25	43	42	24
9	51	53	12	13	51	∞	16
64	12	15	61	61	6	7	47

The Moon.

37	70	29	70	21	62	12	14	41
16	28	70	30	71	12	53	14	46
47	20	11	7	31	72	22	35	15
16	48	68	40	81	32	62	25	56
57	17	49	29	7	66	33	65	25
26	58	40	56	31	42	74	34	66
53	27	59	10	51	2	41	75	35
36	68	19	60	11	65	43	44	76
77	28	20	69	61	12	25	60	5

By adding up each column of these squares, the characteristic number of the planet is invariably obtained, and by finding the explanation of this number among the hieroglyphs of the Tarot, the significance of all those figures, whether triangular, square, or transverse, which are formed by the numbers, may be obtained. The result will be a complete and profound knowledge of all the allegories and all the mysteries concealed by the ancients under the symbol of each planet, or rather of each personification of their influences, whether celestial or human, on all the events of life.

The religious and Kabbalistical key of the Tarot will be now given in technical verses after the fashion of the ancient lawgivers.

1. א. All things announce a conscious, active cause,
2. ב. Vivific Oneness based on number's laws;
3. ג. Who all containing is by nought confined,
4. ד. And all preceding hath no bound assign'd.
5. ה. This only Lord should man adore alone,
6. ו. Who doth true doctrine to pure hearts make known.
7. ז. But acts of faith require a single chief,
8. ח. Whence we proclaim one altar, law, belief;
9. ט. The changeless God will never change their base.
10. י. He rules our days and dooms through every phase.
11. כ. His mercy's wealth, which vice to nought will bring,
12. ל. His people promises a future King.
13. מ. The tomb's a path which to new worlds ascends,
And life through all subsists, death only ends.

Pure, sacred, steadfast truths we here repeat
The venerated numbers thus complete!

14. נ. The angel blest doth calm and moderate,
15. ס. The evil is the fiend of pride and hate.
16. ע. God doth the lightning and the fire subdue;
17. פ. He rules the dewy eve and evening dew;
18. צ. The watchful moon He sets to guard our heights,
19. ק. His sun's the source of life's renewed delights.
20. ר. His breath revivifies the dust of graves.

20 or 21. ש. Where crowds descend who are of lust the slaves;

21 or 22. ת. The mercy-seat He covers with His crown,
And on the cherubs pours His glory down.

By means of this purely dogmatic explanation the figures the Kabbalistic alphabet of the Tarot will be already understood, but a table of its variations, according to divers Kabbalistic Jews, may also be added.

Aleph. Being, spirit, man or god; the intelligible object; unity, the mother of numbers; the primitive substance.

All these ideas are hieroglyphically expressed by the figure of the JUGGLER, who, in other words, represents the active principle in the oneness of divine and human autocracy. His body and arms form the letter א, the prototype of sacred letters; he wears a nimbus about his head in the form of ∞, the symbol of life and the universal spirit; in front of him there are swords, cups, and pantacles, and he lifts the miraculous rod towards heaven. He has a juvenile aspect and curly hair, like Apollo or Mercury; he has a smile of assurance on his lips, and the glance of intelligence in his eyes.

2 *Beth. The house of God and of man, the sanctuary, the law, the gnosis, the Kabbalah, the occult church, the duad, woman, the mother.*

Hieroglyph of the Tarot, vulgarly called the Female Pope, POPE JOAN; a woman crowned with a tiara, with the horns of the moon or Isis, the head surrounded by a veil, the solar cross on her breast, and supporting on her knees an open book, which she partly conceals beneath her mantle.

The author of a pretended history of Pope Joan has discovered and adapted to his thesis, for good or for bad, two curious and ancient figures of the female pope or sovereign priestess of the Tarot, who is endowed in them with all the attributes of Isis; in the one she holds and caresses her son Horus, in the other she has long and flowing hair. She is seated between the two columns of the duad, wears a sun with four rays on her breast, sets one hand on a book, and makes with the other the sign of sacerdotal esoterism, *i.e.*, she opens only three fingers, keeping the rest clasped to signify mystery; the veil is behind her head, and on either side of her seat there is a sea whereon the flowers of the lotus are blooming. I deeply commiserate the unfortunate scholar who declines to see anything in this time-honoured symbol but a monumental portrait of his so-called Pope Joan.

In other Tarots the duad is symbolized by the Greek Juno, with one hand elevated towards heaven and one pointing to the earth, as if formulating by this gesture the unique and dualistic dogma which is the base of magic, and opens the marvellous symbols of the Hermetic Emerald Table.

3. *Ghimel. The Word, the triad, plenitude, fruitfulness, nature, generation in the three worlds, the Mercury of the Sages.*

Symbol, THE EMPRESS, a winged woman, crowned, seated, and bearing on the top of her sceptre the globe of the world; she has the eagle, image of life and the soul, as her sign. This figure is the Greek Venus-Urania, which was represented by St John in his Apocalypse as the woman clothed with the sun, crowned with twelve stars, and having the moon beneath her feet. It is the mystical quintessence of the triad, spirituality, immortality, the Queen of Heaven.

4. *Daleth. The door of government among the Easterns, initiation, the Tetragram, the tetrad, the philosophical cross, the cubic stone, or the base thereof.*

Hieroglyph, THE EMPEROR, a sovereign whose body represents a right-angled triangle, and the legs a cross, the image of the Athanor of the philosophers.

5. *He. Indication, demonstration, instruction, law, symbolism, philosophy, the woman, religion, the diabolical or angelical pentagram.*

Hieroglyph, THE POPE, or supreme hierophant. In the more modern Tarots this sign is replaced by the image of Jupiter. The grand hierophant seated between the two columns of Hermes and Solomon makes the sign of esoterism, and supports himself on a cross with three horizontals of triangular form. Before him are two inferior ministers on their knees, so that having above him the capitols of the two columns, and below him the two heads of his ministers, he is the centre of the quinary, and represents the divine Pentagram, of which he affords the complete significance. In effect, the pillars are necessity, or law, the heads liberty, or action. From each pillar to each head a line may be drawn, and two lines from each pillar to each of the two heads. Thus will be obtained a square divided by a cross into four triangles, and in the centre of this cross will be the supreme hierophant, we had almost said like the garden spider in the centre of its web, if such a comparison were appropriate to the things of truth, glory, and light.

6. *Vau. Concatenation, interlacement, lingam, the shaft of Eros, entanglement, union, embrace, strife, labour, antagonism, combination, equilibrium, the week of creation.*

Hieroglyph, man between vice and virtue. Above him beams the Sun of Truth, and in this sun is Love bending his bow and threatening vice with the shaft. In the order of the ten Sephiroth, this symbol corresponds to Tiphereth, that is, to idealism and beauty. The number six represents the antagonism of the two triads, that is, of absolute negation and absolute affirmation; it is, consequently, the number of labour and liberty; and for this reason it corresponds to moral beauty and glory.

7. *Dzain. Weapon, sword, cherub's sword of fire, sacred septenary, triumph, royalty, priesthood, spirit and form, the three powers of the triad and their four relations.*

Hieroglyph, a cubic chariot with four pillars, and an azure and starry drapery. Within the chariot, and between the four pillars, a victor crowned with a circle, from which rise and radiate three golden pentagrams. The victor has three superposed squares on his cuirass; he has the Urim and Thummim of the sovereign sacrificer on his shoulders, represented by the two crescents of the moon in Gedulah and Geburah; he holds in his hand a sceptre surmounted by a globe, a square, and a triangle; his attitude is proud and calm. To the chariot is harnessed a double sphinx, that is to say, two sphinxes joined at the buttocks; one of them turns his head, so that they look in the same direction. The one turning his head is black, the other is white. On the square which forms the front of the chariot there is the winged disc of the Egyptians surmounting the lingam of India. This symbol is perhaps the most beautiful and complete of all those which compose the clavicula of the Tarot.

8. *Cheth. Balance, attraction and repulsion, life, terror, promise, and menace, the tetragram with its reflection, the double stauros, the tetrad multiplied by the duad.*

Hieroglyph, JUSTICE, with sword and balance.

9. *Teth. Good, hatred of evil, morality, wisdom, initiation.*

Hieroglyph, a sage supported on his staff and holding a lamp in front of him; he is wholly enveloped in his mantle. His inscription is THE HERMIT OR CAPUCHIN, because of his oriental hood; but his real name is PRUDENCE, and he completes thus the four cardinal virtues which appeared imperfect to Court de Gebelin and Etteilla.

10. *Jod. Cause, manifestation, praise, manly honour, phallus, virile fecundity, the paternal sceptre, Malchut, the Kingdom of God, the visible universe, the natural principle of supernatural things.*

Hieroglyph, THE WHEEL OF FORTUNE, that is, the cosmic wheel of Ezekiel, with a Hermanubis ascending on the right, a Typhon descending on the left, a Sphinx equilibrating both, and holding a sword in its lion-like claws. This admirable symbol was disfigured by Etteilla, who replaced Typhon by a man, Hermanubis by a mouse, and the Sphinx by an ape, an allegory in all respects worthy of the Kabbalah of Etteilla.

11. *Caph. The hand in the act of grasping and holding, synthetic unity, perfect man, virility, age of reason.*

Hieroglyph, STRENGTH, a woman crowned with the vital ∞, closing calmly and without effort the jaws of a raging lion.

12. *Lamed. Example, teaching, public lesson, accomplishment, sacrifice, spirit emancipated from matter.*

A man hanging by one foot and his hands tied behind his back, so that his body forms a triangle with inverted point, and his legs a cross above the triangle. The gibbet has the shape of a Hebrew Tau; the two trees which support it have each of them six lopped branches. The cross, superposed on an inverted triangle, is an alchemical symbol known to all adepts, and represents the accomplishment of the *magnum opus*. This personage who is thus hanging is therefore the adept, bound by his engagements, and with his feet turned towards heaven, signifying spiritualization; it is also the antique Prometheus, expiating by an immortal agony the penalty of his glorious theft. It is vulgarly the traitor Judas, and his execution menaces those who reveal the Great Arcanum.

13. *Mem. The firmament of Jupiter and Mars, domination and power, new birth, creation, and destruction, immortality through change, transmutation.*

Hieroglyph, DEATH, reaping crowned heads in a pasture where men are growing.

14. *Nun. The firmament of the sun, temperatures, seasons, motion, revolutions of life, which is ever new and ever the same, harmony of composites, forms tempered by equilibrium.*

Hieroglyph, TEMPERANCE, an angel, bearing the sign of the sun on her forehead, and the square and triangle on her bosom, pours from one ewer into another the two essences which compose the elixir of life.

15. *Samech. The firmament of Mercury, occult science, magic, commerce, eloquence, mystery, moral strength, the astral serpent, physical life, perpetual motion, the great magic agent.*

Hieroglyph, THE DEVIL, the goat of Mendes, or the Baphomet of the Templars, with all his pantheistic attributes.

This is the only hieroglyph which Etteilla perfectly understood and properly interpreted.

16. *Ayin. The firmament of the Moon, deteriorations, subversions, changes, weaknesses, destruction by antagonism.*

Hieroglyph, a tower struck by lightning, probably that of Babel. Two individuals, doubtless Nimrod and his false prophet, or minister, are precipitated from top to bottom of the ruins. One of them in his fall represents perfectly the letter ע, ayin.

17. *Phe. The firmament of the Soul, outpouring of thought, moral influence of the idea on forms, immortality, nature one and deathless in diversity, eternal fruitfulness.*

Hieroglyph, THE BURNING STAR and eternal youth, an admirable allegory:—A naked woman, who represents at once Truth, Nature, and Wisdom unveiled, inclines two urns towards the earth, and pours out fire and water thereon; above her head glitters the Septenary, circling round an eight-pointed star, that of Venus—symbol of peace and love; the plants of earth flourish round the woman, and on one has alighted the butterfly of Psyche, emblem of the soul, replaced in some copies of the sacred book by a bird, a more Egyptian and probably more ancient symbol. This figure is analogous to many Hermetic symbols, and has its correspondence with the Burning Star of Masonic initiates, which gives expression to most of the mysteries of the secret Rosicrucian doctrine.

18. *Tsade. The elements, the visible world, reflected light, material forms, symbolism, mysteries, esotericism, doctrine, hierarchic distribution of the light of occultism.*

Hieroglyph, THE MOON, dew falling, a crab in the water, rising towards the earth, a dog and a wolf tied to the foot of two towers and barking at the moon, a path lost in the distance, and sprinkled with drops of blood.

19. *Quoph. Compounds, the head, the Apex, the Prince of Heaven, the true light, truth, the Holy City, Philosophical Gold.*

Hieroglyph, a radiant SUN, and two naked children joining hands in a fortified enclosure. In other Tarots, it is a spinner unwinding destinies; in others, again, a naked child mounted on a white horse, and displaying a scarlet standard.

20. *Resch. The vegetative, the generative power of the earth, the Great Arcanum of eternal life.*

Hieroglyph, THE JUDGMENT. A genius sounds a trumpet, and the dead rise from their graves. These dead people, thus brought back to life, are a man, a woman, and a child—the triad of human life.

21. *Schin. The sensitive, flesh, fatality, blindness, matter left to itself, eternal life.*

Hieroglyph, THE FOOL. A man in fool's dress wandering aimlessly, burdened with a wallet carried behind him, and doubtless full of his follies and vices. His disordered clothes reveal that which should be concealed, and he is attacked by a tiger without knowing how to avoid it or defend himself.

22. *Thau. The microcosmos, the Absolute, the universal synthesis, and the universal science.*

Hieroglyph, Kether, or the Kabbalistic CROWN, between the four mysterious animals; in the midst of the Crown is Truth, holding a magic wand in each hand.[1]

Such are the twenty-two keys of the Tarot which explain all its numbers. Thus, the juggler, or key of the unities, explains the four aces with their quadruple progressive signification in the three worlds and in the First Cause. Thus, the ace of deniers or of the circle, is the soul of the world; the ace of swords is militant intelligence: the ace of cups is loving intelligence; the ace of clubs is creative intelligence.

[1] See Note 39.

They are also the principles of motion, progress, productiveness, and virility. Each number multiplied by a key gives another number, which, explained in its turn by the keys, completes the philosophical and religious revelation contained in every sign. As each of the fifty-six cards can be multiplied by the twenty-two keys in turn, a series of combinations results which gives all the most astonishing consequences of revelation and of light. It is a truly philosophical machine which prevents the mind from going astray, even while leaving it its own initiative and freedom; it is mathematics in their application to the absolute, the alliance of the real and the ideal, a lottery of thoughts, all of which are rigorously exact, like numbers; in fine, it is perhaps at once the simplest and grandest thing ever conceived by human genius.

If we now take a Tarot and join by fours all the cards comprising the Wheel or ROTA of William Postel, if we place the four aces, the four duads, &c., together, we shall have ten packets of cards providing the hieroglyphical explanation of the triangle of the Divine Names on the scale of the denary which we give on page 286. They may be then read off as follows, comparing each number with its corresponding Sephiroth.

יהוה

Four letters of the name all names combining—

      1. Keter. The four aces.

See on God's crown four mystic gems are shining!

      2. Chocmah. The four twos.

His wisdom's fount a four-fold stream diffuses.

      3. Binah. The four threes.

His intellect its four-fold proof produces.

      4. Chesed. The four fours.

Four bounties ever from His mercy rise.

      5. Geburah. The four fives.

Four times His rigour will four faults chastise.

> 6. Tiphereth.   The four sixes.
>
> His beauty is revealed by four pure rays.
>
> 7. Netsah.   The four sevens.
>
> As oft His conquest in our songs we praise.
>
> 8. Hod.   The four eights.
>
> Four times He triumphs in His life eternal.
>
> 9. Jesod.   The four nines.
>
> Foundations four support His throne supernal.
>
> 10. Malchut.   The four tens.
>
> Four times the same His single realm declare,
> Like to the gems that star His crown of glory rare!

By this simple arrangement the Kabbalistic sense of each plate may be seen. Thus, for example, the five of clubs signifies rigorously the Geburah of Jod, that is, the justice of the Creator and the wrath of man; the seven of cups the victory of mercy, or the triumph of woman; the eight of swords signifies conflict or eternal equilibrium; and so on for the rest. We may thus understand how the ancient pontiffs made use of it to elicit oracles; the plates, drawn by lot, always gave a new Kabbalistic sense rigorously exact in its combination, which alone was fortuitous; and as the faith of the ancients attributed nothing to chance, they read the responses of Providence in the Tarot, which were called by the Hebrews Theraph or Theraphim, as was perceived first of all by the erudite Gaffarel, one of the accredited magicians of the Cardinal de Richelieu.

As to the trump cards they may be explained by a final couplet:—

> King, Queen, Knight, Knave.
> The bridegroom, youth, and child, then all the human race—
> Thy path by these degrees back to the One retrace.

The ten Sephiroth and twenty-two Tarots form what the Kabbalists call the thirty-two paths of the absolute science.

The method of reading the hieroglyphs of the Tarot is to arrange them either in a square or triangle, placing the even numbers in opposition and conciliating them with the uneven. Four signs always express the absolute in any order whatsoever, and are interpreted by a fifth. Thus the solution of all magical questions is that of the Pentagram, and all antinomies are explained by harmonious unity.

So disposed, the Tarot is a veritable oracle, and answers all possible questions with more clearness and accuracy than the Android of Albertus Magnus; so that a prisoner devoid of books, had he only a Tarot of which he knew how to make use, could, in a few years, acquire a universal science, and converse with an unequalled doctrine and inexhaustible eloquence. This wheel, in fact, is the true key of the oratorical art, and of the great art of Raymond Lully; it is the true secret of the transmutation of darkness into light; it is the first and most important of all the arcana of the *magnum opus*. By means of this universal key of symbolism all the allegories of India, Egypt, and Judea are made intelligible; the Apocalypse of St John is a Kabbalistic book, the sense of which is exactly indicated by the figures and numbers of the Urim, Thummim, Theraphim, and Ephod, all summarized and completed by the Tarot; the sanctuaries of eld are no longer full of mysteries, and the signification of the objects of the Hebrew cultus may for the first time be understood. As a fact, who does not recognise in the golden table, crowned and supported by cherubim, which covered the ark of the covenant and served as the propitiatory, the same symbols as in the twenty-first key of the Tarot? The ark was a hieroglyphical synthesis of the whole Kabbalistic doctrine; it contained the rod, or blossoming staff, of Aaron; the He, or cup, the gomor, which held the manna; the two tables of the law, a symbol analogous to that of the sword of justice; and the manna contained in the gomor, four objects which wonderfully interpret the letters of the divine Tetragram.

We have ourselves discovered, in a sufficiently extraordinary manner, a sixteenth-century medal, which is a key to the Tarot. We scarcely know whether we should confess that this medal, and the place where it was to be found, were shewn to us in a dream by the divine Paracelsus; however this may be, the medal is in our possession. On one side it represents the juggler, in a German costume of the period, holding his girdle in one hand, and the Pentagram in the other. On the table in front of him, between an open book and a clasped purse, he has ten deniers or talismans arranged in two lines of three each, and in a square of four; the legs of the table form two ה, and those of the juggler two inverted ד. The back of the medal contains the letters of the alphabet disposed within a magic square, after the following manner:—

A	B	C	D	E
F	G	H	I	K
L	N	M	O	P
Q	R	S	T	V
X	V	Z	N	

It will be seen that this alphabet has only twenty-two letters, the V and N being repeated, and that they are arranged in four quinaries, with a tetrad for basis and key. The four final letters are two combinations of the duad and triad, and read Kabbalistically they form the word Azoth, by ascribing to the configuration of the letters their value in primitive Hebrew, and by reckoning N as א, Z as it is in Roman characters, V as the Hebrew ו Vau, which between two vowels, or letters of the value of vowels, is pronounced O, and X as the primitive Tau, which was precisely of this shape. The whole Tarot is therefore explained in this wonderful medal, truly worthy of Paracelsus, which we submit for the examination of antiquaries. The letters disposed by four times five are summarized by the word אZות, analogous to those of the Tetragram and INRI, and containing all the mysteries of the Kabbalah.

Vestiges of the Tarot are found among all nations of the world. The Italian version is the most faithful and the best preserved, but it may be even further improved by precious indications borrowed from the Spanish game, which still preserves the chief primitive signs; the two of cups, for example, in the *Naïbi*, is completely Egyptian, and we there see two antique vases, having handles formed by two ibises, superposed on a cow; in the same cards a unicorn is found in the centre of the four of deniers; the three of cups shows us the figure of Isis issuing from a vase; while from two other vases two ibises come forth, one bearing a crown for the goddess, the other a lotus, which he appears to be offering to her. The four aces bear the image of the sacred hieratic serpent, and, in certain games, the double triangle of Solomon, is depicted in place of the symbolic unicorn.

The German Tarots are more mutilated, and little beyond the numbers of the keys can be found in them, these being crowded with pantagruelian figures. The Chinese Tarot preserves several emblems; the deniers and swords may be easily recognised, but it would be more difficult to identify the cups and clubs.

It was at the epoch of the Gnostic and Manichæan heresies that the Tarot was lost to the Church, and it was at the same period that the meaning of the divine Apocalypse also perished. It was no longer known that the seven seals of this Kabbalistic book are seven pantacles to be explained by the analogies of the numbers, characters, and symbols of the Tarot. Thus the universal tradition of the one religion was for an instant broken, the darkness of doubt spread over the whole earth, and to the uninitiated it appeared that true Catholicism, universal revelation, had for a moment vanished. The explanation of the work of St John by the signs of the Kabbalah will be a perfectly new revelation.

The most curious and most complete key to the Tarot is found in the monumental work of Kircher on Egypt. It is the reproduction of an Isiac table which once belonged to the celebrated Cardinal Bembo. This table was of copper with figures in enamel; it has unfortunately been lost, but Kircher's copy is faithful, and this learned Jesuit divined that it contained the hieroglyphic key of the sacred alphabets, though he was unable to pursue his interpretation. The Bembine tablet is divided into three equal compartments; above are the twelve celestial houses, below the twelve laborious stations of the year, in the centre the twenty-one sacred signs corresponding to the sacred letters. In the heart of the central region is the figure of the pantomorphic INYX, the emblem of the universal being, corresponding to the Hebrew *Jod*—that unique letter from which all others are derived. Around the INYX, there is the Ophionian triad, corresponding to the three mother letters of the Egyptian and Hebrew alphabet; on the right are the two ibimorphous and Serapian triads; on the left is the Nepthean triad and that also of Hecate, symbols of active and passive, volatile and fixed, fructifying fire and generating water. Each pair of triads combined with the centre gives a septenary; the centre itself contains one. Thus, the three septenaries give the absolute numeral of the three worlds, and the complete number of primitive letters to which a complementary sign is added, as the zero to the nine numeral symbols.

The alphabet of Thoth is the original of our Tarot only in an indirect manner. The latter, as it has been preserved to us, is of Jewish origin, and the symbolical figures are not older than the reign of Charles VII. Jacquemin Gringonneur's game of cards is the first Tarot with which we are acquainted, but it reproduces symbols of the highest antiquity. The game itself was an attempt on the part of some astrologer of the period to restore the monarch to reason by means of this Key of oracles, the answers to which, resulting from the diverse combination of the signs, are always exact like mathematics and proportioned like the harmonies of nature. But in order to utilize this instrument of science and reason, one must already be truly reasonable, and the unfortunate king, relapsed into a second childhood, saw only an infant's toy in the pictures of Gringonneur, and turned the mysterious alphabet of the Kabbalah into a game of cards.

This is the end of this publication.

Any remaining blank pages are for our book binding requirements and are blank on purpose.

To search thousands of interesting publications like this one, please remember to visit our website at:

http://www.kessinger.net

CPSIA information can be obtained at www.ICGtesting.com
Printed in the USA
LVOW05*1633090714

393594LV00020B/695/P